Knee High and Living Large
The World According To Me

by Li'l Penny Hardaway
with Stacy Wall

L'l Penny

#1/2

Crown Publishers, Inc. / New York

MY LAWYER
CHECKED ALL THIS STUFF OUT.
— LP

Copyright © 1997 by Nike, Inc.

Published by Crown Publishers, Inc., 201 East 50th Street, New York, New York 10022. Member of the Crown Publishing Group.
Random House, Inc. New York, Toronto, London, Sydney, Auckland
http://www.randomhouse.com/

CROWN and colophon are trademarks of Crown Publishers, Inc.

Design by Gary Koepke and Laura Forde except for the cover

Printed in China

Library of Congress Cataloging-in-Publication Data

Wall, Stacy.
  Knee high and livin' large: the world according to me / by Li'l Penny Hardaway with Stacy Wall. — 1st ed.
      p. cm.
  1. Advertising—Sporting goods.   2. Advertising—United States.   3. Li'l Penny (Fictitious character)   4. Nike (Firm).   I. Title.
HF6161.S65W35 1997
659.1'968876323—dc21   97-30924
                                                            CIP

ISBN 0-609-60236-5

10 9 8 7 6 5 4 3 2 1

First Edition

CHECK ME OUT. I'M IN THE LIBRARY OF CONGRESS.

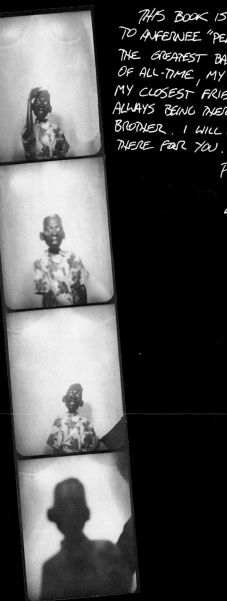

THIS BOOK IS DEDICATED
TO ANFERNEE "PENNY" HARDAWAY,
THE GREATEST BASKETBALL PLAYER
OF ALL-TIME, MY MAIN MAN AND
MY CLOSEST FRIEND. THANKS FOR
ALWAYS BEING THERE FOR ME MY
BROTHER. I WILL ALWAYS BE
THERE FOR YOU.

PEACE

L.P.

I would like to thank my agents, Kevin and Carl Poston, the best sports agents in the world, thank you for taking such good care of me, and the entire PSP Family (Professional Sports Planning). Where would I be without you guys?

And of course, I want to thank my mother and my grandmother for their support.

Much love goes out to Greg Moore, Steve Miller, Randy "Big Daddy" Wade, Kathy Dawson, Sherea McKenzie, and Jackie Day.

I love you always Tyra Banks, you are the sunshine of my life.

And thanks to Jaleel White, Kevin Garnett, Randolph Childress, Rex Chapman, and George Gervin for all the inspiration, thanks to Spike Lee, Joe Pytka, Phil Morrison, and Chuck Willis for directing my commercials, and thanks to Chuck Willis for also editing all my commercials. Thanks to Choppy. Thanks to Phil Knight, Tom Clarke, and Mark Thomashow and all the other good folks at Nike who treat me so very well. Thanks to Dan Wieden and Bill Davenport, and to all the good folks at Wieden & Kennedy, I say thanks for taking me higher. Thanks to the talented Gary Koepke, Laura Forde, Adam Schechter, Joy Sikorski, and Niloufer Moochhala for making my book look so good. Thanks to Chris Rock, a comedic genius and a genuinely nice man, where would I be without you, huh Chris? M5, you are all brilliant, thanks for all of your encouragement and support, and thanks for putting up with all of my shenanigans. Much appreciation to Tom and Martha and Madison and k. t. Blessington. A shout out to Ernest Lupinacci, Donna Portaro, Beth Harding, Andrew Christou, Young Kim— feel better my man, Arty Tan, Hank Perlman—thanks for all the barbecues, Jon Goldberg— thanks for writing my movie, Steve Elliott—thanks for listening, Winton Sweum—thanks for decorating my house, David Helm— thanks for cutting my hair and keeping it "old fashioned." A special thanks to John "The Commish" Helm, and Paul Goldman, Alice, and good old Rid. Thanks to the lovely Anne Wall for appearing in my movie and for being so beautiful and talented. Thank you Nas for loaning me your music. Thanks to Kurtis Blow, much love and respect to the Orlando Magic Dancers, and thanks to Jeff and Stephanie Jacobs and Scott Greenberg. My sincere appreciation to Crown Publishers, especially Steve Ross. Jordan Benjamin Ross, thanks for being even mo Li'l. Susan Scharf, thanks for the nutritional advice and support, Chip "Chip" Gibson, thanks for giving a guy a break, Andrew Martin, you kill me man (and now it's on record, so you better not try anything, "Bro"), thanks to Alan Ross for turning me on to Mozart. Naomi and Sam, thank you. And high fives to Peter Kuper, Tony Stonier, Roger Scholl, David and Andrew Scharf (known in Precinct 5 as the Scharf Brothers), Linda and Jennifer (oh, you two!) Alexia Brue, and you-know-who. Thanks to David Black for promoting me, thanks to the City of Memphis, special thanks to Terence Trent D'Arby, musical genius, thanks to Wake Forest University, Krispy Kreme Doughnuts, and all the legends of the ABA.

Thanks to Max, Adrienne and Margy Koepke, thank yous and hand shakes to Emma Lineberger, Helen Wall, Eddie Guy, Guy Gonzales, Don

Rose, Alan Weber, Jean-Michel Basquiat, Robert Frank, Dan Winters, John Farley, Ed Lynch, Dan Saimo, Michael Panella, Emily Woods, Lee Wall, Kent and Susan Wall, Erik Markgraf, Mike Marinelli, Colin Wolf, Johnny Semerad, Chris Hellman, Sophie Scoufraras, John Young, Evil Knievel, Jeff Foster, Shepard Fairey, Chad Goldman, and Carolyn and Duke Wieden. Special thanks and shout-outs to Slam Magazine, the Lobster Club, Crew Cuts Editorial, The Jewel of India, the city of New Orleans, and a very special thanks and great loads of respect to the Mighty Bunton League, the greatest fantasy basketball league in the world. Thanks to Tim Reardon, Cindy Lewellen, Andy Berndt, Jared Gosler, Thomas Harvey, Chris Noble, and all of the people behind the scenes. Derek Ruddy, thanks for teaching me how to play the guitar. Thanks to Mark Crosby, Chris Browder, Lee Wall, Luna, Fleau, Daniela and Sophie Elliott, John and Elizabeth Siegel, Mary and John and Emily McDonald, James Bolen, Sterling Charles, and Darin Spease. Thanks to Mark Todd and Esther Watson for the fabulous portraits, thanks to Steve Marsel, thanks to Raymond McKinney and Sean Riley, keep pinging and ponging, thanks to Randy Sosin, much respect to Paul Goldman, Alice Buchanan, and good old Rid. Respect to Bob Costas, Dave Doernberg, Superchunk, Lane Wurster and all of the Chapel Hill crew, thanks to John Sweeney, thanks to Coach Dave Odom at Wake Forest, thanks to Tim Duncan, thanks to Alan Broce at MTV, thanks to Craig Kilborn, thanks to Curtis Mayfield, Joe McCarthy, James Brown, the Beastie Boys, thanks to John Glazer, much respect and love to Satchel Paige, Len Bias, Mookie Blaylock, Gary Payton, the Bad News Bears, and Domilises Sandwiches in New Orleans. And finally, thanks to John Blessington for getting me out of that sticky legal situation.

RESPECT + LOVE

—LP

From the time he was five, everyone in my Memphis neighborhood knew that someday, Li'l Penny would be famous. And that's because he was always saying it himself. "I'm going to be famous. I'm going to be large. Just like George Gervin," he would say to anyone who would listen. He really thought he would play in the pros, as my running mate, and he was sure we would both end up in the Hall of Fame. But things didn't quite work out the way he planned.

I have been blessed with the ability to play basketball, and although I never sought out fame, fame found out I could play.

LP, on the other hand, had to find his own road to fame. And, as you'll see in this book, he has tried many different ways to get there. Pro basketball in Madagascar. A movie with Tyra Banks. A rap album. You'll see. All of that and more.

But he really hit the big time when I allowed him to appear in my Nike commercials.

I still regret that decision. But, you know, looking back, we've had fun, and even at the age of 25, LP is still pretty much the same little brother who used to tag along with me everywhere I went in Memphis. And he will still tell anyone who will listen how famous he is and how famous he will become.

And now he's written a book. A book I will not be reading. I don't need to. For 25 years now, I've had to put up with LP's loud mouth. I know all about the stories in the book, because LP never shuts up. In fact, he's been calling me late at night and reading aloud from his book on my answering machine. He's annoying. I see enough of him.

I don't want to read his book.

But you know what? Even with all of his faults, he has always been a loyal friend.

I trust him. He's my brother. And plus, he's fun to hang around. I mean no one, no one, can make me laugh like LP.

So, enjoy the book. Maybe you'll get to know LP a little better. But please, read with caution. LP likes to exaggerate. I tend to believe about half of what he says.

Peace,

Anfernee "Penny" Hardaway

WHO SAYS I CAN"T WRITE? A NOTE TO THE DOUBTING
THOMASES.

Many people have cast many a doubt over my ability
to write a book. Well, those people have a lot
in common with many of Shaquille O'Neal's free throws.
THEY'RE MISGUIDED.

After months spent cloistered out at my lake
house, hammering away on this old Bell & Howell,
I can finally present my highly anticipated
first tome. Yes, "Knee High and Living Large.
The World According to Me" is certainly a work
of genius. I'm telling you, it's a page turner.

But the question remains. Will it win the Pulitzer?

Well, I have succeeded in everything else I have
ever done and I do not intend to start failing now.
In fact, "I Do Not Intend to Start Failing Now"
is the working title of my second book, a self-help
book, which will be published shortly after "The World
According to Me" becomes a permanent fixture on the
best seller list, thank you very much.

That's right, LP is prolific, and I plan on building
a body of work that will make Danielle Steele feel
lazy.

But many people have asked me, "LP, why atypewriter?
Why not a computer?"

Well the answer to that question is simple. I'm old school.
I have no interest in going cyber. In fact, I consider
the Internet the CB radio of the nineties. I'm no
Doogie Howser. Plus, the typewriter makes me sound
like a news-man.

So, in closing, and at the risk of over-statement,
let me just say, 'MY BOOK MAY WELL BE THE GREATEST
SINGLE WORK OF LITERATURE EVER PUBLISHED.'

Publish or Perish,

LP Von Hardaway

THIS BOOK WAS THE FIRST BOOK
I WROTE. NO ONE
LIKED IT.

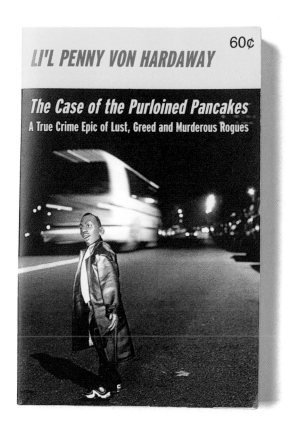

penny

old school

new school

B2222

I am exactly one year younger, to the day,
to the minute, to the second, younger than
my older brother Penny, the world's greatest
basketball player. When I was born, I was
so little that my Moms called up the tv show
That's Incredible to see if they would do a
story on the world's smallest baby. I mean
I was small. And I'm still small. But I don't
let it bother me, or get me down, because that's
not how I was raised. When we were little,
Penny wouldn't let anyone kid me about my size.
And my grandmother always told me to be proud of
who I was, no matter what. And I am. I figure
you have to eat the cheese sandwiches life
packs in your picnic, and so I just move on, ~~chasin~~
chasing my goals and living large. And I'm proud
of all that I have achieved. I've become ~~█████~~
a real star, and like JR Rider said after he
won the dunk contest, "I just have to love
myself for that."

I have fond memories of my days in ~~█████~~
Memphis. Penny and I always reminisce back
to the good old days, when we were just shorties
coming up, and we try to get back to ~~Memphis~~
whenever# we can.   MEMPHIS

MEMPHIS SHORTIES

I still love taking baths. Rub a dub dub LP in the tub!

Look at me. I was so little.

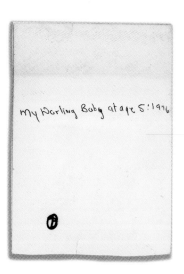

My Darling Baby at age 5: 1976

Check out Penny with the butterfly collar.
He was 5 years old.

I was trying to eat the camera.

Please do not use
essay book for drawings!

L. P. Hardaway
Mrs. Allen's Class
April 14, 1984

(A-)

Birdhouses

How do birds decide who gets to
live in the birdhouses? There are
not that many birdhouses in the
world, there are a lot of birds and
this makes me wonder. If I was
a bird I would like to live in a
birdhouse, and I would fly around
to look for a nice one. Birds do
not fight over who gets to live there.
Maybe they don't like the houses and
they like trees better. Maybe birds
are nicer than people and less greedy.
I don't know. Who knows?
Mother Nature knows and she ain't talking!

                                    L. P.

is not

When I was 11, I was a star pupil.

17

Sophomores

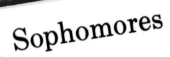

Stephanie Allen
Shelley Burleson
Monica Carpenter
Calvin Claxton
Robert Conger

Fatasia Conway
Kendrick Conway
Sonya Cooper
Tonya Cooper
Marsha Ewing

Brian Fowler
Raquel Green
Sherae Griffith
Anfernee Hardaway
Li'l Penny Hardaway

William Jackson
Pearl Lewis
Shericka Murphy
Lorie Needham
Avery Nickson

Melissa Oester

PENNY ↓

ME. ↑

HIGH SCHOOL
Penny and I both played for the Treadwell High
basketball team. I ran the point, and Penny and I were
an unstoppable combination.

19

When the time came for college, Penny and I made different choices.
Penny, of course, went to Memphis State, where he became, as they say,
the man. But I was only recruited by two schools, Eastern Michigan and
Wake Forest. Now, playing at Eastern Michigan, George Gervin's alma
mater, was tempting, but in the end I decided Wake Forest was the best
program for me. So I left home, moved to Winston-Salem, NC, and became a
Demon Deacon.

My career at Wake Forest was frustrating. I did not get the kind of
playing time I thought I deserved. The one game I did start, I lit up
Athletes in Action for 22 points and 12 assists. People in Winston still
talk about that game. But in ACC games I rode the pine. My best friend on
the team, a guy I still talk to all the time, was Randolph Childress. He
encouraged me to keep my head up and just work on my game, and so in
practices I really worked hard. This impressed my coach, Dave Odom, and

PENNY AT MEMPHIS STATE   FRESHMAN YEAR, VS. NC STATE

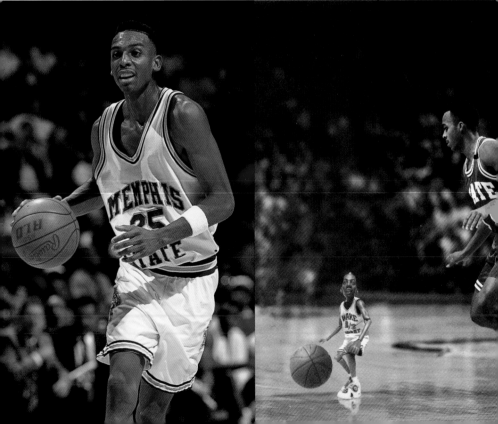

after practice one night he told me I was going to see some real playing time against Duke in a nationally televised game the next day. But, as fate would have it, I fell off a stool at a Krispy Kreme doughnut shop the morning of the game, and I twisted my knee really badly.

And I never really recovered from my doughnut injury.

I had a lackluster college career, but I still had the dream to play pro basketball, and so, after college, I put together a highlight reel of some of my better high school games and my one great game against Athletes in Action, and I sent the tape to every professional team I could think of. I was even willing to play in Italy or Greece (even Turkey), but no one seemed interested, at home or abroad. My height was a true liability.

On the other hand, Penny's career was taking off, and he really wanted me to move down to Orlando to be his business manager.

WAKE TEAM PICTURE.   THAT'S ME IN THE MIDDLE.

In an unfortunate side-note, Li'l Penny Hardaway, who was slated to see significant time against Duke, is out with a knee injury sustained in a fall from a stool at the Stratford Road Krispy Kreme Doughnut Shop this morning.

MY APARTMENT BUILDING IS THE TALL ONE, THIRD FROM THE RIGHT. IT'S TOO HOT HERE AND I CAN'T FIND A CHEESEBURGER ANYWHERE ON THE ISLAND.

-LP

MADAGASCAR MEMORIES

But one day, when I had just about given up hope, I got a letter from a team in Madagascar, called the Antananarivo Lemurs. They had seen my tape, they were impressed with my quickness and showmanship, and they were offering me a tryout.

I didn't even know where Madagascar was, but I didn't care. I just knew I had a shot to play pro ball, and so I booked my flight, packed up some things, and made the trip.

I soon found out where Madagascar is. It's an island off the southeastern coast of Africa, and let me tell you, it's about as foreign as a foreign country can be.

My tryout with the Lemurs went really well. My knee felt good, and my skills, compared to most of the Madagascan boys', were far superior. They offered me a contract on the spot, and in my excitement, I signed without really knowing what my life there was going to be like.

Madagascar is a beautiful place, it really is, and my life there was pretty good. I had a beautiful apartment with an ocean view, and the people there were all very nice to me.

On the court, I lit things up. I played some of the best ball of my career, and I became somewhat of a Madagascan national hero. The Lemur fans were nuts about me. And crazy loyal. They even named a street after me. But I never really felt at home, and no matter how well I played, it was clear to me that no NBA team was even paying attention. The Madagascan Pro League — the MPL it is called — was not and is not respected by the NBA scouts. So, as soon as my contract was up, I moved back to Orlando and took Penny up on his business offer.

And so I became Penny's business manager, which led to my appearances in Penny's TV commercials.

LI'L PENNY HARDAWAY
ANTANANARIVO 1993

MY ROOKIE CARD, ISSUED BY A GAS STATION IN MADAGASCAR, IS VERY VERY RARE.

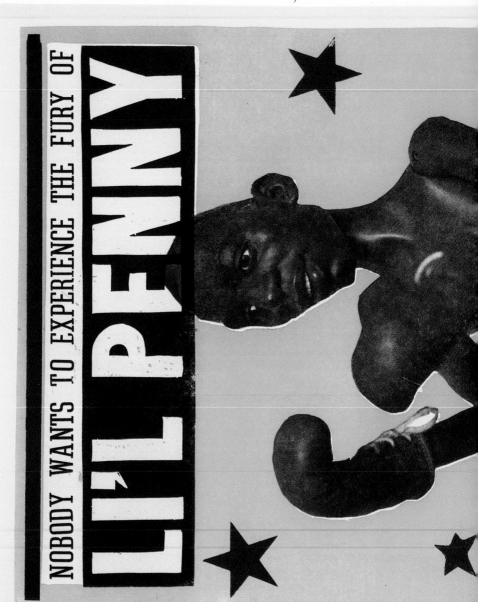

NOBODY WANTS TO EXPERIENCE THE FURY OF

LI'L PENNY

WEET SCIENCE IS A ROUGH BUSINESS, SO I FINALLY AGREED TO GO TO WORK FOR PENNY.

-L.P.

CHRIS "THE ANIMAL" NOBLE

VS.

LI'L PENNY HARDAWAY

GENERAL ADMISSION $10

V.I.P. $30 - RINGSIDE $20 -

THE FASTEST FISTS IN FLORIDA

UNDEFEATED SUPER SUPER ULTRA FLYWEIGHT CHAMPION

© Hatch Show Print

You see, one of my main duties was to review any advertising concepts created for Penny, and decide if they were appropriate and good for Penny's image. I kept my eye on the big picture. Penny is a franchise, and we can't have him running around just selling anything and everything. So I attended all sorts of meetings with companies, ad agencies, and theme restaurants. Lots of theme restaurants. I was tough, I rejected concept after concept. But I wasn't interested in being liked. I wasn't running for office. I was protecting Penny's image.

And one day, I was out in Beaverton, Oregon, sitting in a Nike conference room, listening to some creative director from Nike's ad agency, Weeden & Kenneely, pitch me on a concept for Penny's new shoe. I can't even remember what it was, something about finding a "lucky penny," or something, but I do remember it was terrible.

So in the middle of the meeting, I turned to Phil Knight (Nike's CEO, thank you very much,) and I said, "Phil, we need to talk." So Phil and I left the conference room, and we took a stroll around the Nike Campus.

During our walk, I expressed to Phil my frustration with the poor conceptual thinking on Penny's Nike ads, and I also told him I had zero respect for his ad agency. I told him they hadn't done a good commercial since "Bo Knows," and then I asked, "Phil, is Penny the next Michael Jordan?" And Phil said, "Yes, LP, what's your point?" And I said, "Well then why are you advertising him like he's the next Alex English?" And Phil Knight laughed and laughed and laughed. And then he said, "LP, you're funny. You're smart. You should be in Penny's ads."

And that's where it all started. It was all Phil Knight's idea. (And I should add, I mean no harm to Alex English in retelling this story. Alex English was a terrific player, a prolific scorer, and a fine actor. I mean it. Rent <u>Amazing Grace and Chuck</u> sometime. Alex English carries that film.)

So, anyway, I agreed to co-star with Penny in some ads. I figured we would make two or three, win some Clios and be done with it. But the ads caught on, and pretty soon I became the man you see today. An American pop culture phenomenon. I'm large.

CARL POSTON ↓

MY AGENTS WITH ME THE DAY I SIGNED MY LUCRATIVE NIKE DEAL.

KEVIN POSTON ↙

From the Desk of
Li'l Penny Von Hardaway

Dear Phil,

After thinking about it over the weekend and weighing the pros
and the cons, I have decided to accept your offer to appear
with Penny in his Nike ads. But I do have a few demands.

First of all, I must have complete creative control. I've
seen some of the early scripts for me and Penny and I must re-
spectfully say, they stink. I just need to be allowed
to ad-lib, free associate, make things up as I go, and
Nike will certainly then get some fierce commercials.

Also, the commercials must be focused on Penny and his
prowess on the court. I will be Penny's sidekick, but
every effort must be made to keep my magnetic personality
from stealing the proverbial show.

And of course, I must be paid a substantial sum of money.

So, until I see you again,

Keep yourself cool

LP Hardaway

P.S.- A substantial sum of money.

MY DEBUT - LOCKER ROOM

And my first commercial with Penny was titled,
"Locker Room." As you can see, the original script
was pretty bad, but my ad libs and rewrites turned it
into pure marketing genius.

We rehearsed "Locker Room" for like eight weeks.
Penny really wanted the commercial to be perfect, so
we even took the commercial on the road, performing
at community theaters during the summer, working out
all the dynamics, making sure all the performances
were tight. When Penny and I felt we had finally
crafted the greatest commercial ever conceived, we
moved to a sound stage to try and capture our magic on
film. And the shoot was grueling. We filmed for eight
days. Penny and I both had stunt doubles and body

doubles, and Penny had a hand model stand in for him
during the close-ups of him tying his shoes. All the
other guys who are in the Locker Room as extras are
classically trained Shakespearean actors, except for
the white guy who walks behind Penny during the end of
the spot, who happens to be an audio-animatronic
robot. We just could not find an actor who walked with
the precise slow gait so common to white power
forwards, so we had to make some movie magic.

ADVENTURES?
I DON'T HAVE ADVENTURES

Nike
The Adventures of Li'l Penny
"Locker Room"

OPEN ON ANFERNEE HARDAWAY AND LI'L PENNY SITTING IN THE
LOCKER ROOM. LI'L PENNY IS WHISTLING A HAPPY TUNE.

I DO NOT WHISTLE.

                    LP
    Excuse me Anfernee, but what team are you playing
    tonight?

                    PENNY
    We are playing the Minnesota ball club. A fine
    team.

THIS SCRIPT IS BORING. IT NEEDS MORE SPICE!

                    LP
    Well, good luck Penny. Good luck.

                    PENNY
    Thanks Li'l Penny.

                    LP
    And Penny, please tell my friend Kevin Garnett
    hello for me.

                    PENNY
    Okay, I will do that Li'l Penny.

                    LP
    Thanks Penny.

← BORING!

KEVIN,
I'M NOT APPROVING THIS. I'M INTO THE IDEA OF
DOING ADS, BUT COME ON MAN, THIS IS TERRIBLE.
YOU TELL THE AD AGENCY TO GET THEIR ACT TOGETHER.
L.P.

29

more locker room

After the filming and the editing, we thought the
commercial was good, but we had no idea what Joe Public
would think. But "Locker Room" was a huge success.
Everyone was running around saying "Can you do that for
a brother?" It sort of became a catch phrase, and for a
while, I got really sick and tired of everyone asking
me to say it over and over again. But now, I realize my
great contribution to the pop culture lexicon, and I'm
thinking of starting a charitable organization, The Can
You Do That For a Brother Foundation, next year.

The Orlando Magic uniform I wear in "Locker Room" bears
the number 1/2. It was the ad agency's idea. I didn't
think this was too funny, but Penny thought it was
hilarious.

The chalkboard in the background says "Helm!" at the
bottom. This is a little inside joke to David Helm, my
good friend in Richmond, who used to cut my hair.

The director of "Locker Room" asked me to sing a little
something at the start of the commercial, like I was
listening to a song on my headphones. So I did. I sang a
few bars from my own song, "Don't Forget the Funk,"
which was also the name of an album I was promoting at
the time.

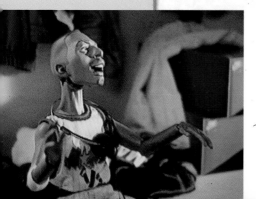

LOS LOBOS

SPANISH FOR THE WOLVES.

NEW JACK RHUMBA

★★ ★★★ • CALL TYRA

DON'T FORGET N'OUBLIEZ PAS
THE FUNK!!

NON DIMENTICARE

WHEN I WAS A LITTLE ~~KID~~ BOY,
MY MOMS SHE SAID TO ME.
REMEMBER WHO YOU ARE,
AND LEARN THE ~~▓▓▓▓▓▓~~, FAMILY TREE?
BE HEALTHY AND BE STRONG.
AND PLEASE STAY OFF THE JUNK
AND LASTLY PLEASE MY SON,
DO NOT FORGET THE FUNK.
<u>CHORUS</u>
NO MATTER WHAT YOU DO YOU DON'T FORGET
THE FUNK. DO NOT FORSAKE THE FUNK.

THE GREAT THELONIOUS MONK
DID NOT FORGET THE FUNK.
THE MIGHTY TITANIC SUNK, — THE CAPTAIN FORGOT
THE FUNK.
LIKE THE ELEPHANT HAS TRUNK
WE ALL MUST HAVE THE FUNK ★★

<u>BRIDGE</u>
A PENNY DUNK
A MYSTERIOUS CLUNK.
LIKE FRED SANFORD HAD
JUNK
WE ALL MUST HAVE THE
FUNK

FARCESSEN NICHT

NO OLVIDE

LP's

I CAME UP WITH
THE ORIGINAL LYRICS TO
"DON'T FORGET THE FUNK"
IN A HOTEL ROOM IN
PORTLAND, OREGON.
I WAS PARTICULARLY
PLEASED WITH THE FRED
SANFORD LINE.

MY CD WAS A BIG HIT IN BELGIUM.

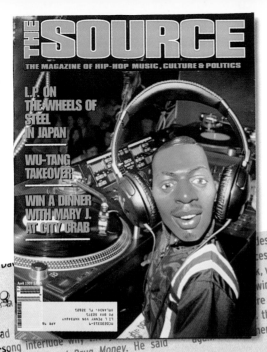

THE SOURCE

THE MAGAZINE OF HIP-HOP MUSIC, CULTURE & POLITICS

L.P. ON THE WHEELS OF STEEL IN JAPAN

WU-TANG TAKEOVER

WIN A DINNER WITH MARY J. AT CITY CRAB

April 1997 $3.95

...describes being between a rock ...es (the two women he loves), ...k, which speeds up the shuffling ...winklings from Slick Rick's "Hey ...re both sure to propel the Lost ... the soundtrack for dancefloors ...er. And isn't that all we ask for?

BRETT JOHNSON

...s lead ...een-song interlude why ... again ... was titled *Legal Drug Money*. He said ...thing to the effect that instead of slinging ...ock like he used to, he's now making paper ...anufacturing the universal opiate—music. ...hough the rap-crack game analogy is a ...led concept, it somehow is so appropriate ...plaining the LB's success.

L'IL PENNY

Don't Forget the Funk

LP Records
Production: artist

Don't Forget the Funk? How about the melody? The rhymes. Anything listenable? Li'l Penny has created an incoherent mess of a debut album, an amateurish effort, chock full of clichéd samples (Funky Drummer?), brain dead beats, and a title song which rhymes the word "funk" with "mysterious clunk." Consider this lyric from "Tyra Interlude," a track L.P. has described as "a slow jam." "Lounging on the sofa/Getting down to business/Got a cough drop in my mouth/smells of lemon eucalyptus." Please. In closing, don't forget the funk, but by all means, forget this debut.

SETH ZARKIN

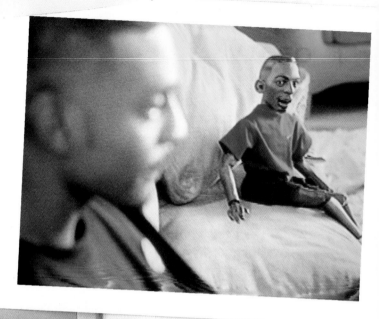

THE STUPENDOUS AND AWARD WINNING "LIVING ROOM" SPOT.

"Living Room" won several Clios.
Several. (The Clio is not the
Oscar of advertising, it's more
like the People's Choice Awards,
buxkuk but anyway, it's something.)
in faCT,many in the advertising
community say"Living Room" is the
finest commercial ever filmed.
   I really liked filming it, because
I got togive Penny the business
about his bad commercal and his
bad couch. By the way, the idea
for Penny's fake commercial in this
spot came from all those boring
advertising meetings I used to
have to sit in. And believe me,
I saw some concepts just as bad
as the one inttthe commercial.

Penny really loved the glitter suit.
   It was later sold at a charity
auction for $5,000.

Penny does have a couch made of
imitation leather, and it does
stick to my legs sometimes, so
I ad-libbed and it became my second
catch phrase.

"HEY PENNY, IS THIS
COUCH REAL LEATHER?
CAUSE ITS STICKING
TO MY LEG."

CATCH PHRASE
#2

PARTY

"House Party" is a based on a true
story. I did throw a heck
of a party once at Penny's house
while he was on the road, and
he did call in during the party,
and I did get in a little hot water.
Speaking of hot water, some a rather
steamy hot tub scenes were edited
out of this commercial by the network
censors.

Penny is really good in this
commerc l. His line about "my
sloppy friends" cracks me up every time
I see it. Penny can act.

"Oh Sheila" by Ready for the World
is the song in "party."

The woman who kisses me is an actress.
We had nothing but a professional
relationship on the shoot, does
even though Tyra, to this day, does
not believe me.

The line about Tai Chi was originally,
"I had to change the channel to
"I had to calm myself down," but
VH1 just to calm myself down," but
it was rewritten for legal reasons.

HOUSE PARTY !

The man who walks behind me without
his shirt is the director of the
commercial, Phil Morrison. What
a nut he is. At one point during
the shoot, he demanded that no one
be allowed to look directly at him,
and he directed the entire commercial
from behind a silk screen.

"I CAN'T HEAR YOU.
I'M DRIVING THROUGH
A TUNNEL."

↗ CATCH PHRASE #4

TYRA

This commercial holds a special place in my heart, for it was on the set of "Car," that I met the love of my life, Tyra Banks. Tyra and I hit it off immediately, and everyone could sense the on-screen chemistry between us. I really do not want to provide any more intimate details of our special moments in my book. I will save that for my Barbara Walters interview.

And I've never been the choreographer for the Magic Dancers. Once again, the ad agency's idea of comedy.

ROMANCE!

The [illegible] Airlines Boeing 767. Long-range. Wide-body.
Unsurpassed comfort. The sleek, silver bird flies on, FULL OF GERMS

TYRA BABY,

ONCE AGAIN I HAVE CAUGHT A COLD.
THANKS TO THE AIRLINE INDUSTRY'S
GENIUS POLICY OF RE-CIRCULATING THE
AIR UP THERE. THERE MUST BE SOME
SORT OF WHOOPING COUGH CONVENTION
IN PHOENIX, BECAUSE MY PLANE WAS
LIKE A SCENE OUT OF "OUTBREAK."
PEOPLE WERE HACKING AND SNEEZING
AND WHEEZING AND SPITTING. ONE OF
THE STEWARDESSES WAS HOLDING HER
STOMACH AND MUMBLING, "NO ONE WANTS
WHAT I'VE GOT." I'LL TELL YOU, IT'S
A WONDER I'M STILL ALIVE.
LOVE XXXO
LP

767-300 LuxuryLiner
PETRI DISH

MISS TYRA BANKS
[address blacked out]
NEW YORK, NY
10011

THE BEST
DENTIST OFFICE
WAITING ROOM
OF ALL-TIME.!
ALL-TIME!

NOTHiNG BUT BiKiNiS

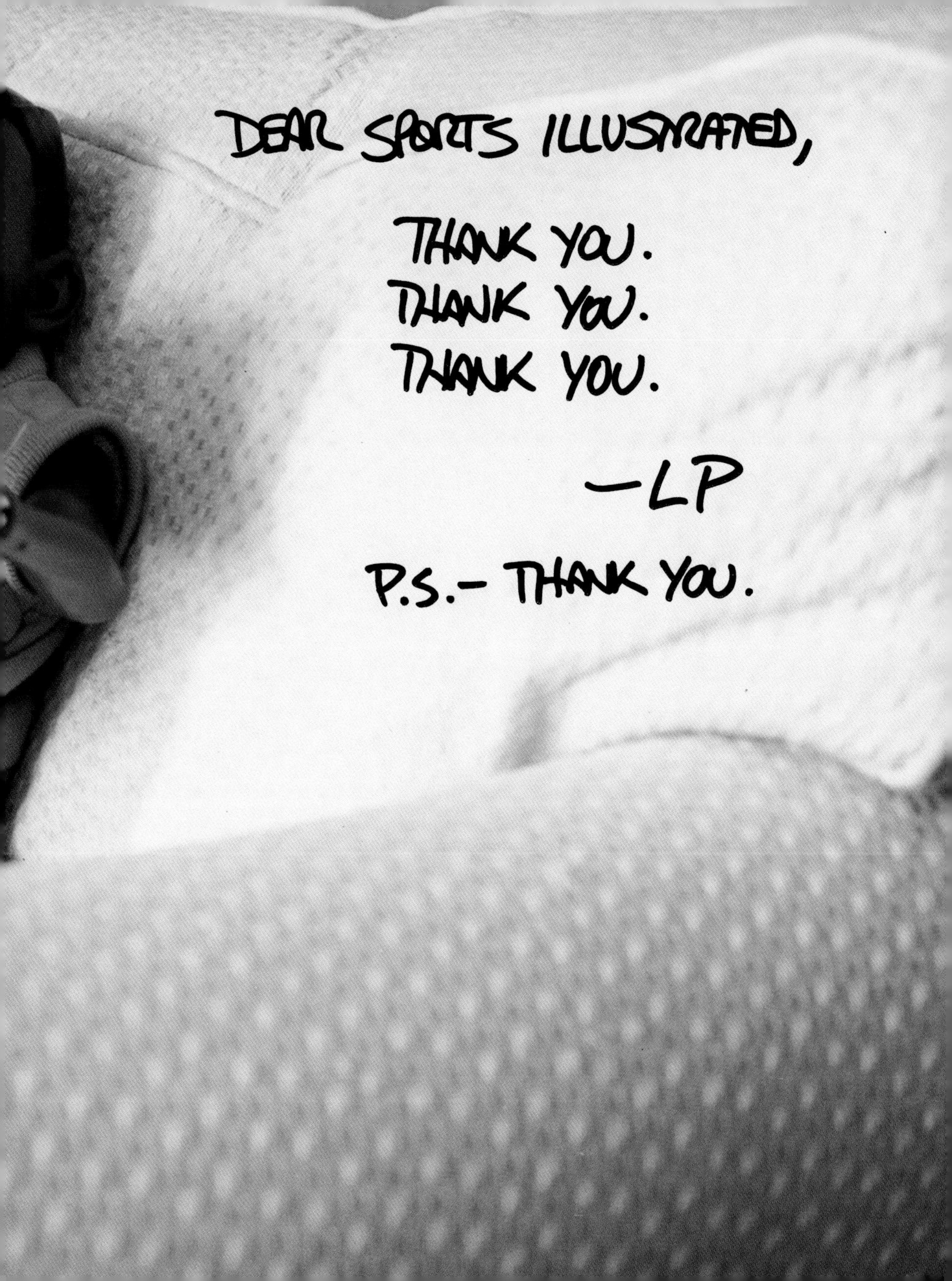

DEAR SPORTS ILLUSTRATED,

THANK YOU.
THANK YOU.
THANK YOU.

—LP

P.S.— THANK YOU.

and when Tyra told him she didn't speak Portuguese, things really got out of hand. But hey, that's modeling.

DC: And do you try and see all of her fashion shows?

LP: Well, I don't really enjoy the fashion scene. It's all a little too pretentious for me. I'm a man of simple means. I mean, sure, I sleep in a hyperbaric chamber, but I'm basically a t-shirt man. But I try to support Tyra, and I catch a

bond Tyra and I have to a magazine? To Barbara Walters? So we keep it private as best we can. We smile for the paparazzi, and make a few appearances, and we let the tabloids write what they want to. And we don't let the media glare bother us. I mean, who know what they're going to write. Last week, some tabloid said I was dating Jewel.

DC: You're kidding.

LP: No, I'm not kidding. How could I make

DC: "Who eez the leetle man." That's great.

LP: Embarrassing. But Penny has it worse than me as far as the fame trip goes. Everybody knows Penny. And Penny is internationally large. You should have seen him in Japan. If he ran for King of Japan he would win. People in Japan are naming their kids Penny and stuff. It's crazy. And speaking of Japan, I have an album coming out this spring, "LP, Kicking it Live at Budokan."

DC: Like Cheap Trick?

LP: Who?

DC: I want to get back to what you were saying before about electric cars. Do you really believe that?

LP: Yes I believe it. I mean, it's like my friend Hank Perlman said to me, "We have an electric car rolling around on Mars. Mars! And Detroit says we can't have electric cars on Earth?" I'm telling you, it's a conspiracy. But you know, I have a cousin who invented a weaving process for towels that you can't see or feel, but that sets off a security alarm whenever a towel is taken from a hotel.

DC: Yeah?

LP: And his patent was bought and buried. Buried by a towel company.

DC: They buried it?

LP: Yes. They sell a lot of replacement towels to hotels.

DC: Oh, I get it.

LP: It's just business.

DC: Speaking of business, show business that is, how are things going with your movie career?

LP: Oh, swimmingly, just swimmingly. "Double Action 2, the Widowmaker," is in pre-production now. I'm currently filming a re-make of "The Fish that Saved Pittsburgh." And last week, Tyra and I wrapped up our wacky romantic comedy, "Two Sandwiches Shy of a Picnic." My friend Goldy wrote the script, and it's brilliant. I mean, it makes "Chasing Amy" look like an Afterschool Special.

DC: And Spike directed?

LP: Oh yes, it's a Spike Lee joint. And Tyra is so good in this movie. We've got more chemistry than Dow Pharmaceutical.

DC: The early buzz on "Sandwiches" is really good.

LP: Well, I always generate good buzz. LP was born with good buzz. I'm like a honeybee on wheels! ∎

> ## "WELL, I ALWAYS GENERATE GOOD BUZZ. LP WAS BORN WITH GOOD BUZZ. I'M LIKE A HONEYBEE ON WHEELS!"

few shows, but you know, during the basketball season, I'm on the road with Penny. And Tyra understands that. She gives me my space. She does her thing, and I do mine.

DC: Your relationship has been so public. How have you handled it?

LP: The relationship? Or the media?

DC: The media.

LP: Well, you know, as Thelonious Monk once said, "Talking about music is like dancing about architecture."

DC: So you don't talk about your relationship?

LP: No I really don't. How could I explain the

this stuff up? (laughs) But it's cool. We laugh about it. Tyra and I are solid, the media cannot destroy what we have.

DC: Is fame a burden?

LP: Hell no. I love my fame. I bask in it. I wear it well. But I know it's not going to always be like this. Some people don't know who the hell I am. When I was in France with Tyra, all these French people kept asking her "Who eez the leetle man?" I mean no one knew me over there. And it was sobering it really was. But I can handle it. I'm going to ride this fame thing out, and then I will move on.

interview

July 1997

THE HARDEST WORKING MAN IN SHOE BUSINESS
LI'L PENNY AS SOUL BROTHER #2

45

SPIKE

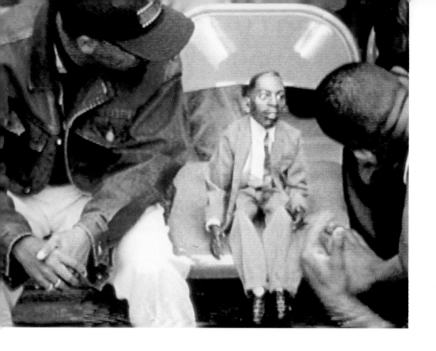

Spike Lee was a pleasure to work with in this commercial,
which after months of research and deliberation, I simply
titled "Spike." And Penny shines in this spot. He really made
everyone think we shot this during a real game. But we didn't.
We re-created a game-like atmosphere on a sound stage.

One interesting note. At the beginning of the commercial Spike
is pitching me about being in a movie with him and Tyra.
"Picture this, a romantic comedy, starring you and Tyra Banks.
It would be a smash." Well, this line was not scripted. Spike
did not know the cameras were running, and his actual "pitch"
to me was so funny, I decided to include it in the final edit.

Spike did not know the cameras were runni
"pitch" to me was so funny, I decided t

Thanks for a great shoot. You're a tremendous talent. Peace, Spike Lee

IN "OLD SCHOOL DREAM" PENNY
AND I PLAYED WITH A RED,
WHITE + BLUE BALL IN HONOR
OF THE ABA. AND PENNY STARTS
OFF WITH A FINGER-ROLL IN
OLD SCHOOL HONOR OF
THE ICEMAN, GEORGE
GERVIN.

"BASKETBALL" BY KURTIS BLOW
HAS ALWAYS BEEN ONE OF MY
FAVORITE THINGS.

DREAM

"Old School Dream" is one of my
favorite spots, because I finally
got to show off my talents on
the court. Reporters are always
asking me, "LP, can you pix play?"
 It's insulting and annoying.
 This commercial showed the xxxkx
world I truly have the skills
to pay the bills. Anyone who
ever saw me play in college or
in Madagascar knows, I haVE HANDLES.
 I can push the rock. As I said
in SLAM Magazine, when I'm running
the point I'm kk like the second
coming of Maurice Cheeks. I set
the table, baby.

"HEY TYRA. YOU LEFT YOUR
TOOTHBRUSH AT MY HOUSE."

↑
CATCH PHRASE
#3

"DOUBLE ACTION"

I asked my old friend Kevin Garnett if he would appear
with me and Penny in the spot called "Movie." He agreed
and we all had a great time on the set. I was mixing my
album, Don't Forget the Funk, at the time, so we filmed
in my recording studio at my house. The talented Nas let
us use his great song, "If I Ruled the World" for the
commercial, and in an incredibly savvy cross-marketing
venture, Nike agreed to let us show a clip from our
action flick, Double Action. Available now on LP Home
Video.

Penny and I wrote the script for Double Action while we
were on the road, just killing time on planes and in
hotel rooms. The script was the talk of Hollywood. A
major bidding war broke out for the rights to what
everyone recognized was a valuable action franchise.
Double Action was a huge hit in overseas markets, but in
the States, the critics completely missed the point of
the film.

Nothing could have stopped me from starring in Double
Action. I was born to play the rogue cop. In fact, I was
supposed to play the Will Smith role in Independence Day,
but I turned it down to make Double Action instead.

I did all of my own stunts in the movie, and I also got
to showcase my karate skills. And working on the movie
was great fun. Joe Pytka directed Double Action and it is
really far superior to any of his other films.

The sequel Double Action 2. The Widowmaker, is slated for
a summer '99 release.

DOUBLE ACTION — THIS TIME, IT'S PERSONAL.

THIS SCENE WAS VERY DANGEROUS TO FILM, BUT PENNY AND I
INSISTED ON DOING OUR OWN STUNTS!

IF THE ACADEMY DOESN'T RECOGNIZE
DOUBLE ACTION, WE HAVE
A PROBLEM.

obby Van, Ruta
enry Wilcoxon.
tifyingly boring
s on a space voy-
ckering.
h) C-92m. ***
n, Judy Geeson,
l, Simon Oates,
nen investigates
ty on an island
cting population.
mystery-thriller,
. Based on the
me name.▼
m. **½ D: Oli-
Frank Whaley,
n, Kyle Mac-
s Burkley, Josh
ichael Wincott,
ensmore, Will
aul Williams,
m, Billy Vera,
ssion of famed
to fame, and
in Stone proves
ghts and sounds
, the rock and
nd early '70s),
e lead . . . but
n't know very
than when the
sses also tend
appears briefly
[R]▼●
61) 80m. *½
onald Woods,
, Midge Ware,
oward, Merle
plot a bank
the cast; also
TO LIVE.▼
78m. *½ D:
res, Charles
Leon Janney,
ey, Kenneth
lkie gangster
cast as ruth-
e and Cagney
film) as his
e (1962-Ger-
ohrer. Eddie
Kinski, Adi

Wilde's novel, updated to the present: vain, immoral young man (Berger) ceases to grow older, while his portrait ages instead. THE PICTURE OF DORIAN GRAY, released 25 years earlier, is vastly superior. Also known as THE SECRET OF DORIAN GRAY. [R]▼

Do the Right Thing (1989) C-120m. *** D: Spike Lee. Danny Aiello, Ossie Davis, Ruby Dee, Richard Edson, Giancarlo Esposito, Spike Lee, Bill Nunn, John Turturro, Paul Benjamin, John Savage. Idealized, individualistic look at life in the black community of Bedford-Stuyvesant in Brooklyn, where a white-owned pizza parlor flourishes . . . and where circumstance leads to an outbreak of hostilities on a sweltering summer day. Entertaining and provocative, with a much-discussed (and troubling) finale. Writer-director Lee also stars as Mookie, the delivery boy; his real-life sister Joie plays his sister in the film. [R]▼●

Double Action (1996) C-122m *** D: Joe Pytka. Anfernee Hardaway, Li'l Penny Hardaway, Chris Rock, Anne Wall, Flip Wilson, Tyra Banks. Li'l Penny is brilliant as the rogue cop seeking to foil a terrorist basketball plot. Many critics misunderstood this darkly heroic film. [R]

Double Bunk (1960-British) 92m. *½ D: C. M. Pennington-Richards. Ian Carmichael, Janette Scott, Sidney James, Liz Fraser. Slapstick account of Carmichael and Scott navigating their houseboat down the Thames, with predictable sight gags.

Double Con SEE: **Trick Baby**

Double Confession (1950-British) 86m. ** D: Ken Annakin. Derek Farr, Joan Hopkins, Peter Lorre, William Hartnell, Kathleen Harrison, Naunton Wayne. Murky melodrama at a seaside resort: an innocent man tries to set someone else up as a murder suspect in his wife's mysterious death, only to get involved with some real killers.

Double Cross (1941) 66m. *½ D: Albert Kelley. Kane Richmond, Pauline Moore, Wynne Gibson. Mild account of cop seeking to get the goods on criminal gang; nothing unusual.

Double Cross (1949-Italian) 77m. **½ D: Riccardo Freda. Vittorio Gassman,

Strange. O'Connor is w
who seeks to win his s
pose crooked city offi
which doesn't quite con

Double Deal (1984-Au
*½ D: Brian Kavanagh
Angela Punch-McGrego
Warwick Comber, Peter
drama about bored, marri
designer Punch-McGrego
with drifter Comber. Fil

Double Dynamite (1951
ving Cummings, Jr. Fra
Russell, Groucho Marx
Star trio at career
flat comedy was made;
clerk accused of theft.▼

Double Exposure (1944-
liam Berke. Chester Mor
Jane Farrar, Richard Gai
taining saga of girl who
photograph of murder.

Double Exposure SEE: N
White▼

Double Impact (1991)
Sheldon Lettich. Jean-Cla
Geoffrey Lewis, Alan Sca
Cory Everson. Identical
rated at six months when
murder their parents, only
revenge a quarter-century la
attempts to delineate two
of them a gruff cigar-cho
as goofy as one slow-m
studio press material, p
Damme career stretch, ex
charming side of his perso
seen before.'' [R]▼

Double Indemnity (1944
Billy Wilder. Barbara
MacMurray, Edward G.
Hall, Fortunio Bonanova
Wilder-Raymond Chandle
James M. Cain novel) pa
account of insurance sales
coerced into murder plot
wyck and subsequent inves
colleague Robinson. An
classic, with crackling d
out. Remade for TV, and
inspiration for Lawrence
HEAT.▼●

Double Indemnity (1973

To Lil' penny —

To my HomeBoy who Always stay in trouble. May god Bless you with all the women in the world and with all the money in the world

SEE ya IN College NeXt year

your Boy

KEVIN GARNETT WROTE THIS NICE NOTE TO ME FOR MY BOOK. I DON'T GET THE "SEE YOU IN COLLEGE" JOKE, BUT THAT'S KEVIN'S SENSE OF HUMOR FOR YOU.

LI'L PENNY VON HARDAWAY

Master American Visionary

Exhibition opens December 2, 1995 at 1pm

THE CAINE ENGLAND GALLERY

The Caine England Gallery is proud to exclusively represent Li'l Penny Von Hardaway and his wonderful and expensive works of American Folk Art. His large paintings, usually depicting his close friend Anfernee Hardaway in action on the court, have been the cause of much critical discourse and debate on what defines "art" in the late twentieth century. Many critics have labeled his works "laughable" and "amateurish," and a few have even used the words "pathetic," and "miserable abominations," but here at the Caine England Gallery we choose instead to see in Von Hardaway's work a man of unique vision and perspective, a man struggling to find light in the darkness, a man expressing himself with paint.

UNDISCOVERED GENIUS OF THE
MEMPHIS HARDWOOD.

I DID THIS PAINTING, "THE PLAYERS"
ON AN OLD SHUTTER I TOOK FROM
THE HOUSE IN MEMPHIS WHERE
I GREW UP.

→ LP

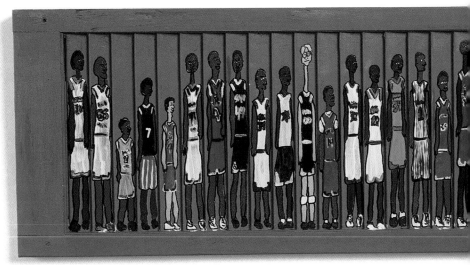

↑
KING
REX!

↑
ICEMAN

↑
KG

↗
PENNY.

IT'S ONE OF MY EARLIER
WORKS, BUT I'M STILL
PROUD OF IT.
— LP

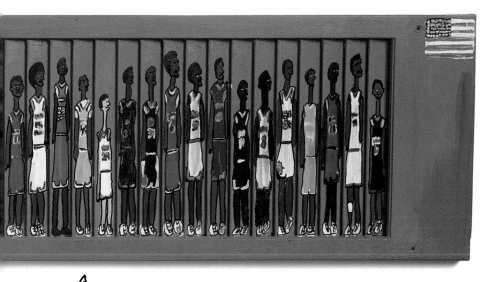

↑
RANDOLPH
CHILDRESS

IF YOU CAN, TRY TO IDENTIFY
ALL THE PLAYERS ON THE
SHUTTER. IT'S DIFFICULT
BUT IT CAN BE DONE!
— LP

63

FIRST BALLOT! NO QUESTION

SPEECH FOR PENNY"S INDUCTION INTO THE BASKETBALL HALL O FAME

Ladies and Gents,

Thank you so very much for attending Penny's ceremony.

I NEED A BETTER JOKE HERE. MAYBE SOMETH ABOUT THE FOOL

As I look out on the parking lot, I can't help but wonder what Dr. Naismith would think of all the rocket cars and all the modern things here in the year 2025.

But I digress. As President of the United States, my schedule is quite hectic, but of course I made time to fly in for Penny's day, and it is good to be back in the USA after the long economic conference in France. Ah yes, the States, where I must say, my popularity ratings are soaring. Yes, abolishing the stock market was a controversial action, but I think we can now all see the wisdom of my moves. And speaking of moves, we are here today to honor a man of many moves.
Yes, the greatest player of all time, Penny Hardaway!!!!!
(PAUSE FOR TREMENDOUS OVATION)
Fourteen World Championships in a row. 102 points in one game. 17 MVP Awards. Leading the league in scoring 17 years in a row. You cannot deny the stats, but to truly understyand and appreciate Penny, we must look past the numbers.
LOOK PAST THE STATS. GO AHEAD, LOOK PAST EM.
Penny had, and still has, as anyone who has visited his palatial estate on the Moon Colony can attest, charisma.

He electrified the crowd. He loved the fans. He loved the game. He still loves the game. Oh sure, Penny and I both have quibbles with the modern game. The anti-gravity court in Utah is an abomination, but today is not a day for quibbling. Today is aday of celebration. For today we honor Penny Hardaway!!!!!!!!!!!!!!
(PAUSE FOR 10 MINUTRE STANDING OVATION AND BALOON DROP)
(CUE BRASS BAND)
And so, as I stand here before the recently re-named Anfernee Hardaway Basketball Hall of Fame, I salute Penny. The Greatest Player of All-Time!!!!!!!!!!!!

MUCH EMOTION. I MIGHT EVEN START CRYING HERE. MUST REMEMBER TO FIGHT THROUGH THE TEARS.

This is a rough draft, there's always time for revisons .

LP

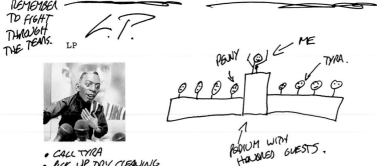

PENNY — *ME* — *TYRA.*

PODIUM WITH HONORED GUESTS.

- CALL TYRA
- PICK UP DRY CLEANING
- WASH CAR
- RESEARCH "WHACE" STORY

Li'l Penny's Traveling All-Stars

Coming soon to a town near you!!!!!!!!!!!

I would ~~be the~~ AS player coach, just like Wes Unseld used
to shake it, ~~And I would run the point.~~ LP Hardaway,
the Madagascan Mo Cheeks.

Penny ~~would~~ dominates and dazzles at the 2. When Penny has
the rock, he creates more space than a Feng Shui master.

At center, ~~I would start my man~~ Rex Chapman. That's right,
King Rex. No team would expect Rex to be my man in the
middle, see? So they would be flummoxed, outfoxed, and before
they knew it, Rex would serve up a couple of long-range
threes after drawing their slow confused center way out
of his element. I'm telling you, I'm a strategic
genius.

My power forward would be Kevin Garnett. And call my man
Brunswick, cause he owns the lane.

At small forward, George "Iceman" Gervin.
Ice is like Harvard. Old school.

And my sixth man? My old college buddy, Randolph Childress.
Randolph's threes are like Maya Angelou's poems.   Deep.

My team would be seriously offensive minded. We would put
up serious numbers!!

—LP!

MY COOKBOOK IS ONLY SOLD IN ENGLAND IN MY RESTAURANT.

CRAWFISH ETOUFEE

CHICKEN ✚ SAUSAGE SHRIMP

★ JAMBALAYA ★★★ ✚

COCHON D☆GRITS

du L.P. DUCK

LAIT! 🍴 GUMBO

O
U
G

MUFFULETTA H

N SHRIMP PO-BOY

ALLIGATOR U CRAWFISH

PIE ✦ T MONICA

CUBAN SANDWICH S

MR. WILLIAMS CRAWFISH

FRIED PIES BOUDIN!

★ ★ ★ ★ ★ ★ ★ ★

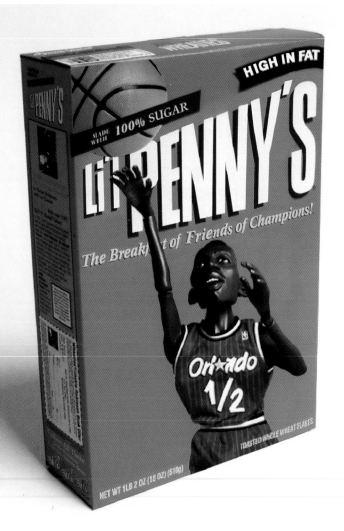

From the Desk of
Li'l Penny Von Hardaway

DEAR CAP'N CRUNCH,

WATCH YOUR BACK.

— LP

PRESENTS

The Li'l Penny Classic Pro-Am Golf Tournament

For the "Can You Do That For A Brother Foundation"

SEPTEMBER 27th & 28th, 1996

TPC at Southwind

THE OPRAH WINFREY SHOW
Transcripts from Li'l Penny's Appearance
February 24, 1997

Winfrey: Well, I'm happy my next guest is here. For such a little guy, he's become a really big TV star, has a reputation for throwing a heck of a party, too. His recent Super Bowl bash was the place to be, honey, I hear. His star-studded guest list included Spike Lee and Tiger Woods and supermodel Tyra Banks. Before we meet this little miniature mega star, let's find out a little more about him and his best friend. Orlando Magic's Penny Hardaway is one of the hottest players in basketball right now. He's also one of the nicest. There's another Penny, Li'l Penny, his pint-sized alter ego.

(Excerpt from Nike commercial)

Winfrey: He's cocky, he's loud, and loves to hang with the stars: Tiger Woods, Tyra Banks and Stevie Wonder were just some of the celebs on his guest list for the party of the year. Now a successful series of Nike commercials is turning this pint-sized dude into a big celebrity. In fact, some fear he's getting a little too big for his Nikes. Looks like Li'l Penny's got the big guy off guard.

(Excerpt from Nike commercial)

Winfrey: Please welcome the littlest big man in professional sports, Li'l Penny.

Li'l Penny: Thank you, Oprah. Thank you very much.

Winfrey: I just want to talk to you for a moment about this fame trip you're on. How did you get so famous?

Li'l Penny: Well, Penny's my main man. So as he got more and more famous, so did I. Now once Penny asked me to appear in one of his Nike commercials, things just blew up. Oh, I'm just out of here, Oprah.

Winfrey: Oh, I see. I see. So it was the Nike thing that did it for you?

Li'l Penny: Yes, it was the Nike thing, but Nike helped me, and I also helped Nike.

Winfrey: OK. I wan—are you—are you dating anyone? Wha—is there anything to the whole Tyra...

Li'l Penny: Well, Oprah, after you and I broke up, things were looking a little rocky. But now I feel—I got a little certain someone in my life. Let's just keep it at that.

Winfrey: A certain someone?

Li'l Penny: Yes, a certain someone.

Winfrey: Would we know who she is?

Li'l Penny: Yes, you would know who she is. You know who Tyra is.

Winfrey: Oh, it is definitely Tyra.

Li'l Penny: It is Tyra. Now don't get jealous on me, Oprah.

Winfrey: We asked NBA basketball stars to tell us what Li'l Penny is really like. And this is what they had to say about you.

Mr. Hardaway: This is Penny Hardaway with the Orlando Magic. I just want to give you a couple of tips on how to handle Li'l Penny. You know, he's very cocky.

Mr. Steve Kerr (Chicago Bulls): Li'l Penny, what's up with the obsession with Tyra Banks?

Mr. Hardaway: He's out of control.

Mr. Horace Grant (Orlando Magic): I've been through it with Li'l Penny. Don't trust him.

Mr. Luc Longley (Chicago Bulls): Li'l Penny, you need to come down a peg. I mean, give up on Tyra Banks. I mean, what—you know, where are you getting this from?

Mr. Hardaway: And, by the way, how do you get on the show anyway? And without me? I don't think that's right. This guy is even bigger than me. Call me, please. I want to say some things. Thanks.

Winfrey: I think you're—I think you're creating a little Penny envy.

Li'l Penny: Well, you know. Penny gets all the money and I have all the funny.

Winfrey: I got it.

Li'l Penny: See what I ...(unintelligible)Oprah. You know, you was talking about Tina Turner's legs. You've got some nice legs yourself.
Winfrey: I know...
Li'l Penny: And I've got a nice view right here. Got a little Sharon Stone action happening, huh?
Winfrey: I guess so from your angle it might be a little...
Li'l Penny: I don't mind. I don't mind.
Winfrey: Anyway, what's your favorite TV show?
Li'l Penny: My favorite TV show? OK, first there's "Homeboys in Outer Space".
Winfrey: "Homeboys in...
Li'l Penny: That's a pretty good show.
Winfrey: Yeah.
Li'l Penny: I like the "Chris Rock Show". That's a pretty good show.
Winfrey: Chris Rock, yeah. Pretty good.
Li'l Penny: But, of course, my favorite show and Penny's and Michael's and everybody else is THE OPRAH WINFREY SHOW.
Winfrey: Yeah! Well, thank you, Li'l Penny. Penny Hardaway—you know what? I—I really want to get him on the show. And I know you could help me do that.
Li'l Penny: I will do whatever I can, Oprah, to help you out.
Winfrey: I appreciate it.
Li'l Penny: All right, hey.
Winfrey: All ri...
Li'l Penny: Anything you need, Ope.

ME AND MY DOG CHOPPY
JANUARY 3, 1996

Choppy is my dog. He's a good dog. Penny and I found Choppy after a game in Cleveland, he was walking outside the Gund arena looking sad and lost, and so we decided to adopt him. He's a good dog, but he has a few quirks.

For example, Choppy loves to eat pancake batter. The vet doesn't approve, but sometimes, when he's been good, we mix up some batter and Choppy has a field day. He laps it up.

Another weird thing about Choppy is that his dog house smells like lemons. We do not know why.

And, whenever Penny's playing a nationally televised game on NBC, Choppy hides under the bed. And he won't come out until the game's over. At first we thought it was nerves. But it turns out, he's just frightened by Bill Walton. If the game's on TNT, Choppy sits right up close to the big screen and barks happily whenever Penny dunks.

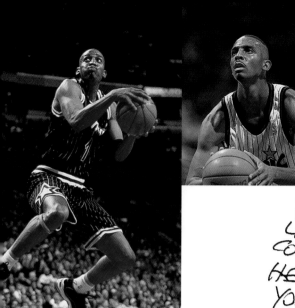

PENNY IS
LIKE A GUIDANCE
COUNSELOR.
HE EXPOSES
YOUR WEAKNESSES!

PENNY'S LIKE THE HARDWARE STORE.
HE HAS ALL THE TOOLS.
PENNY'S LIKE A WARING BLENDER.
HE MIXES IT UP.
PENNY'S LIKE A BENIHANA CHEF.
~~HE HAS MANY DIFFERENT WAYS~~
~~OF CUTTING & SLICING UP~~
~~DEFENSES?~~

PENNY IS THE MAN!

This page is sponsored by Nike

—LP

~~PENNYLAND~~

~~Pennyland will eventually be a slam dunk vacation~~

Pe

PENNYLAND

FUTURE
SITE OF
PENNY-
LAND

PENNYLAND

Pennyland will eventually be a slam dunk
vacation destination for the whole family.
But for now, I¦m inv lved in some sticky
lawsuits with my real estate broker whose
secretary, "mistakenly" deleted the word
"swamp" from the term "swamp land" on
the contracts.

MANY PEOPLE HAVE ASKED ME,
"LP, WHY THE HELL DO YOU HAVE
A SMALL SANDWICH SHOP IN LONDON?"
WELL, I LOVE LONDON, I SPEND A LOT
OF TIME OVER THERE, AND IT SEEMED
I COULD NEVER GET A GOOD SANDWICH.
IN LONDON, A SANDWICH USUALLY
INVOLVES SOME SORT OF A PASTE, OR
CUCUMBERS AND THE BREAD IS USUALLY
STALE, AND I WAS FRUSTRATED BY THIS,
SO I THOUGHT LONDON WOULD APPRECIATE
A GOOD SANDWICH PLACE. SO, I OPENED
LI'L PENNY'S CAFE IN 1995. OUR
SPECIALTY IS A FRIED SHRIMP PO-BOY,
BUT WE ALSO SERVE CHEESEBURGERS,
HOT DOGS, AND GUMBO. AND YOU CAN
GET A KIDNEY PIE, BUT I WOULDN'T
RECOMMEND IT.   LP.

LI'L PENNY'S CAFE
18 STROPPINGFOTTLE ON HEATH

VIBe

LI'L PENNY
A PLAYERS
PLAYER

MAY 1997 $2.99

I REALLY DO NOT LIKE THIS
COVER. I LOOK BAD IN THE
PHOTOGRAPH. I DID NOT GET
ALONG WITH THE PHOTOGRAPHER
AND I TRIED TO GET THE
COVER CHANGED, BUT A REALLY
RUDE DESIGNER OVER THERE
AT VIBE SAID NO.

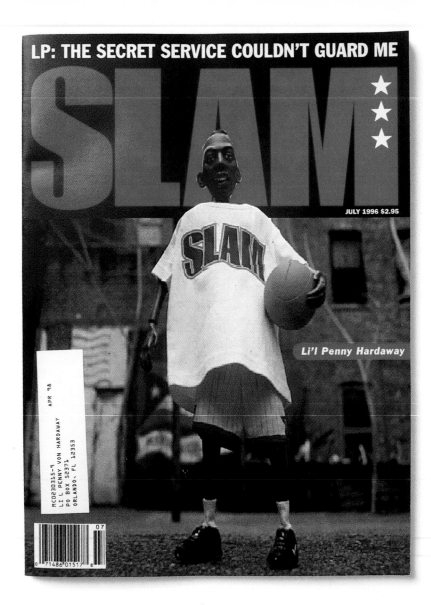

LP: THE SECRET SERVICE COULDN'T GUARD ME

SLAM ★ ★ ★

JULY 1996 $2.95

Li'l Penny Hardaway

LP'S BASKETBALL MOVIE REVIEW

BLUE CHIPS
Of course, a classic. The scene where Penny confronts Nick Nolte about wanting to move back home breaks my heart every time I see it. And Penny's acting is superb throughout this epic film. I often watch *Blue Chips* twice a day. In fact, the only film better than *Blue Chips* is *Double Action*.

DOUBLE ACTION
The scene where Penny is leaving the squad car. You know it. Penny is undercover in his Bunton basketball uniform, and as he leaves the car I say, "Penny, watch your back." And Penny turns to me, as he's walking away from the car in slow motion. (A nice touch.) And he says, "Don't worry about my back LP. My back is tempered steel." Tempered steel! Tempered steel! I'm telling you this movie is a classic for all times, all generations. I own seven copies on laser disc.

HOOP DREAMS
The last line of this movie, from William Gates, is the best end line of all time. Chilling.

THE FISH THAT SAVED PITTSBURGH
This old school classic has something for everyone. Flip Wilson,

Dr. J, Jonathan Winters, (Who plays two roles, the evil owner and the good owner who loves train sets), the Sylvers dancing and singing their way out of a giant box of fish sticks. And classic lines. "What's wrong with twos baby?" "Fruits from the islands. Our islands." Penny and I screen *The Fish* every Thanksgiving. It's a tradition."

THE AIR UP THERE
Smells bad.

FAST BREAK
Lyrical. Gabe Kaplan oozes charisma. Ooozes it.

AMAZING GRACE AND CHUCK
Alex English is smooth in this film. Smooth! And to the kid protesting the nuclear war I say, "Fight the Power! Stick it to the Man!"

HOOSIERS
The only quibble I have with *Hoosiers* is the sappy love story parts with Barbara Hershey. Who needs them. I want to see the team. Running the old picket fence, measuring the rim at the state championship (goose bumps), Dennis Hopper listening to the game on the radio. This movie is a gem. But every time they cut to a scene where Hack-

man and Hershey are walking in some misty Indiana corn field making pie-eyes at each other, I take a bathroom break.

VISION QUEST
Not technically a basketball movie, *Vision Quest* is actually a wrestling movie. But if it had been a basketball movie instead, it would certainly make my all-time classic list. Madonna should have called me.

THE CABLE GUY
Yes. A basketball movie. For that one basketball scene, guaranteed to send me into fits of hysterics every time I see it. One time, Penny had to call a doctor I was laughing so hard. And the Karaoke Jam? I love the Karaoke Jam.

THE HARLEM GLOBETROTTERS GO TO GILLIGAN'S ISLAND
If you have not seen this movie, please, by all means, rent it today. This film combines two great things. The Trotters, and the Castaways. Why this movie is not shown on a constant loop at the Museum of Modern Art is beyond me.

THE ABSENT MINDED PROFESSOR
You must respect the flubber!

The Secretary of State
of the United States of America
hereby requests all whom it may concern to permit the citizen/
national of the United States named herein to pass
without delay or hindrance and in case of need to
give all lawful aid and protection.

Le Secrétaire d'Etat
des Etas-Unis d'Amerique
prie par les présentes toutes autorités compétentes de laisser passer
le citoyen ou ressortissant des Etats-Unis tiulaire du présent passeport,
sans délai ni difficulté, et, en cas de besoin, de lui accorder
toute aide et protection légitimes.

Li'l Penny Hardaway

SIGNATURE OF BEARER/SIGNATURE DU TITULAIRE.

NOT VALID UNTIL SIGNED

UNITED STATES OF AMERICA

PASSPORT	Type/Caté- gorie	Code of issuing / code du pays State USA	PASSPORT NO. / NO. DU PASSPORT

Surname / Nom
HARDAWAY

Given names / Prenoms
LI'L PENNY

Nationality / Nationalité
UNITED STATES OF AMERICA

Date of birth / Date de naissance
3 JAN/JAN 1973

Sex / Sexe   Place of birth / Lieu de naissance
M   **TENNESSEE**

Date of issue / Date de délivrance
21 FEB / FEV 96

Date of expiration / Date d'expiration
20 FEB / FEV 06

Amendments /
Modifications
SEE PAGE

Authority / Autorité
**PASSPORT AGENCY
TENNESSEE**

24

P<USA<HARDAWAY<<LIL' PENNY<<<<<<<<<<<<<<

From the Desk of
Li'l Penny Von Hardaway

Dear Pulitzer People,

Why does one write? Well, it's a calling really. A voice I hear in the wind, a small voice calling to me, "LP, you must tell your story, you must write." And yet, for years, I ignored the voice. But last year, when my agent showed me the giant advance check Crown Books was prepared to offer me to tell my story, I realized the little voice in the wind might have a point.

But I digress.

Let me get with my point. I sincerely believe my book deserves the Pulitzer Prize.

The genius of my book should speak for itself. In fact, you may find this letter redundant, as "Knee High and Living Large. The World According to Me" is probably as we speak being talked up around your headquarters as the clear favorite to win this year, as well it should.

My book has something for everyone. Comedy, tragedy, personal discovery, action shots of Penny, recipes, even a little erotica. What other book offers so much variety in one volume?

So, if you would, just Fedex me the trophy. I have a very busy schedule, and I may have to miss the Awards Show.

Your literary genius,

Li'l Penny

Li'l Penny Von Hardaway

TAXI
WAS A PRETTY GOOD
SHOW. ANDY KAUFMAN - GENIUS.
I LIKE THE CHRIS ROCK SHOW.
AND I REALLY ENJOY
BIOGRAPHY ON A+E, AND
THE FOOD NETWORK. I LOVE
THE FOOD NETWORK. -LP

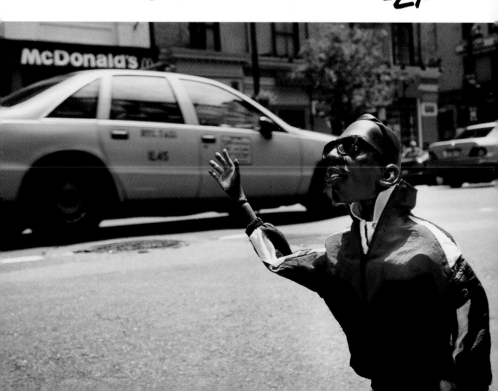

**From the Desk of
Li'l Penny Von Hardaway**

Dear Nike,

Here's your shoe shot.

You're welcome.

Peace,

Li'l Penny

LP

NEW YORK CITY
EMPIRE STATE BUILDING
MAY 1997

HOW DID INSPECTOR DAVENPORT KNOW I would write such a great
book? Because the Inspector is wise to my talents and he is
quite perceptive. All who doubted LP are now in serious need
of moist towelettes to wipe the collective egg from their
collective faces, because as I'm sure you are quite aware by
now, my book is brilliant. It turned out just the way I
planned it. Incisive, witty, titillating, and brazen. Quite
brazen (And with the exception of a few typos and one poten-
tially libelous passage, my book required no re-writes). So
I am quite pleased. But I have no plans to rest on my laurels. The laurels can wait. I've got things to do. I'm con-
sidering taking on Richard Branson in a hot air balloon race
from Madagascar to Memphis. There's talk of performing
"Don't Forget the Funk" unplugged. And Tyra and I have a
wedding to plan. But I'm in no hurry. I take my life day to
day. Some days I feel like taking on the world. Other days,
I'm just looking for the opportunity to spell the word "bar-
becue" in a hot game of Scrabble. But know this. My profits
from this book are going to charity. I don't want to make a
big deal out of that, but I thought you should know. I figure anyone who turned my book upside down to read this last
page must be a real fan, and therefore deserves to know the
truth. And now you do.

Peace

LP